The Tao of Twitter

Changing your life and business 140 characters at a time

Mark W. Schaefer

The Tao of Twitter

ISBN-13: 978-0615437323

Published by Create Space, a division of Amazon Publishing

Contents

Introduction

When I bought my first desktop computer, it came with two sets of instructions.

The first set was a simple color-coded poster to help you know how to plug in the mouse, the keyboard, and the monitor so you could get up and running in a matter of minutes.

The second was a hefty booklet that described the software basics, shortcuts and practical tools to help you really make the device useful.

Studies show that about 60 percent of the people who try Twitter quit after the first week and I'm convinced it's because they never get past the first set of simple instructions: Set up a profile, follow a few celebrities, tweet about "what you're doing now" and see what happens.

Problem is… the second set of instructions doesn't exist.

Until now. And that's why we're here.

Twitter has changed my life and the lives of many of my clients and students. Where so many others have quit or failed, we are enjoying the benefits of the most powerful business networking systems that has ever existed.

It isn't just a cute kiddie-toy or chat function for keeping in touch with friends. With its real-time human-driven results, Twitter has become the networking, information, and search engine of choice for many business professionals. Why? Twitter can help you...

• Attract new audiences and potential customers, partners, and suppliers
• Follow news on your industry, market, competitors, and customers
• Stay on top of the latest research, opinion, insights, and competitive intelligence
• Learn new skills
• Strengthen new and existing business relationships
• Open up low-cost marketing opportunities

Sadly, most people miss this completely because they don't know what I know, and what my students have discovered.

They haven't found the Tao of Twitter.

If you're completely new to Twitter, I recommend that you read this book from start to finish. If you're a pro, feel free to jump around and collect some new ideas along the way!

Discovering the Tao of Twitter

The first tweet I ever received was: "It's 4 a.m."

Obviously Twitter and I did not get off to a good start! Like most people, I thought it was just about the stupidest thing I had ever tried and that first tweet seemed to confirm it.

But I stuck with it because as a consultant and marketing educator, I was determined to learn what the buzz was about. I thought the whole thing was a little silly and maybe even spooky when unknown "followers" just started showing up.

And then I had my "a-ha moment."

I was bored and was playing around on the computer one night when I logged on to Twitter and clicked on a trending topic for #NewFluName. I knew enough by this time to know that these topics represented the most popular real-time conversations in the world. Mildly curious, I clicked to see what was happening. It was a moment I'll never forget.

Remember when the pork industry was having a fit about the swine flu? It thought the name was hurting sales of "the other white meat" and asked the public to call it something else. So thousands of people from around the world were tweeting their contributions -- HILARIOUS new names. Like...

- The Aporkalypse
- Porky's Revenge
- This little piggy went to the bathroom
- Hog Flashes
- Porkenstein
- The Other White Flu
- Mad Sow Disease
- Hamageddon
- ... and my favorite, "Hamthrax"

Yes, it broke the monotony of my evening. But something more important happened. I was witnessing a real-time, global brainstorming session! It dawned on me that at no other time in the history of mankind could that conversation have taken place. It was an awesome moment, an inspiring moment. I began to think about all of the implications for business, for learning... for me.

People sharing, connecting, teaching and entertaining each other in the moment – from every corner of the world. I had caught a glimpse of something wonderful.

Over the next several weeks I witnessed Twitter serve as a powerful news source during the revolutionary activity in Iran. I made my first meaningful business connections. A torrent of links, humor, and insights came rushing at me every day as I learned to surround myself with thought-leaders, teachers, and innovators. I began to realize that Twitter was probably the most dynamic, interesting, and compelling educational tool I had ever seen.

There is a Tao to Twitter. There is a majestic random synergy that holds the potential to impact your life daily... if you know what you're doing. And most people don't know what they're doing. They don't grasp the Tao.

If you dissect any successful Twitter case study, any business benefit, any personal accomplishment that started with a tweet, there is a common theme – a success formula of sorts. The more I have become immersed in the social web, the more I am convinced that this Tao, or formula, is the path to success on Twitter.

Our generation's source of all wisdom -- that would be Wikipedia of course -- defines Tao as a word that **"literally translates as 'way', 'path', or 'route', or sometimes more loosely as 'doctrine' or 'principle,' it is generally used to signify the primordial essence or fundamental aspect of the universe."**

I like that idea. So let's get into this path... this primordial essence. But to best explain it, I need help from a young graduate student and my favorite football team.

The Tao of Twitter in Action

One October evening I was watching my favorite American football team – the Pittsburgh Steelers – and doing a little work-related multi-tasking. I flipped on Twitter and announced through a Twitter message (known as a tweet): "Watching a football game tonight – Go Steelers!"

A few moments later I received a reply from Michelle Chmielewski, (or, @MiChmksi as she is known on Twitter) a graduate student at the University of Pittsburgh. "Watching the game too! Hope we will win!" she tweeted.

Now, I only had a vague idea of who this person was. Although we had "followed" each other, I could not recall ever having any dialogue with her before and certainly had no indication that this random tweet was about to change the course of our lives.

But Michelle knew who I was. Like any smart networker, she had taken care to surround herself with people she could learn from.

Because I was a marketing professional, blogger, and an educator, she had included me in her Twitter tribe and now took this opportunity to reach out and connect on a very human subject -- sports.

About a week later I was surprised and delighted to receive an email from Michelle: "It was nice getting to 'meet' you the other night on Twitter. I really admire what you're doing on your blog, Mark. I am just starting out as a blogger myself. My blog is called "The Observing Participant." Is there any way you could take a look at what I am doing and give me some feedback?"

Of course I was happy to look at her work and what I found astonished me. Michelle was creating innovative video blogs that were unlike anything I had seen. Her content was funny, quirky, and edgy, telling a story in a very entertaining and compelling fashion. I went through post after post and I was convinced I had discovered an amazing talent.

I began to mention her posts in my tweets because I believed in what she was doing and wanted to help her get some exposure. After a few weeks I had the brilliant idea of asking Michelle to actually make one of her charming videos for my new company. Wouldn't that be a unique way to tell MY story and explain what I do?

Michelle said she was interested in the project but felt funny about taking money from her new "mentor." She mentioned that she needed a new high-definition video camera to continue her work so I offered to purchase one for her as a way to help her further her career. She picked out the camera of her choice and my video was on its way. I was so pleased about the success that I wrote a little blog post about it. Although Michelle looks back on this video as being a little crude compared to what she's producing today, it's still on my site as a testament to the beginning of our wonderful friendship.

The Benefits Multiply

Little did I know that the business benefits of this Twitter connection were just starting!

At a networking meeting in Pittsburgh, Michelle met the owner of a start-up company who desperately needed some marketing help. "I know just the guy," she told him and set up a call for me to talk with the entrepreneur.

Now I was a little too busy to take on this business, but I knew just the person who could – my friend Trey Pennington (@treypennington), somebody I had also met through a random tweet. I had recently moved our online relationship into an offline relationship when I met him for lunch in his home state of South Carolina and had learned he was looking for work.

Trey was grateful for the opportunity and followed up with the new business lead in Pittsburgh.

Trey had noticed my blog post about Michelle and was also blown away by her talent. "Can you introduce me," he asked. "I'd like to have her on my show."

Trey has a thought-provoking podcast called "The Marketing Professor" and soon was featuring Michelle and her innovative ideas for using video as a story-telling medium on blogs.

Between the popular blog post, the radio show, and the new traffic to her blog, Michelle's star was rising fast!

As her graduation neared, Michelle was offered a job with a social media software company in Paris. She had never had to consider a life-changing offer like this before and she asked for my advice before responding.

She soon became a successful community manager and her growing company needed a foothold in the United States by hiring a business development manager. "I know just the guy," she said, and recommended that they call me about the opportunity.

My consulting business was strong and I couldn't take on this additional work but recommended that they also talk to Trey, who was already on their radar screen because of Michelle. They met Trey in London and offered him the position.

Over the months Michelle, Trey, and I had opportunities to help and support each other in numerous ways. It could be something as important as a career choice or as simple as pinging Michelle on Skype to get help with a video editing problem.

Going Global

When my wife and I were planning a trip to France, we made a special effort to stay a night in Paris to meet Michelle. While it was a great thrill to finally see her in person, the visit was even more interesting because it coincided with a party she helped plan for a number of bloggers from around the world. Under a bridge. Next to Notre Dame. With champagne.

It was a magical night as I compared notes and exchanged cards with fascinating social media entrepreneurs from Europe, Canada, and South America. One of my new acquaintances was seeking a permanent job in the U.S. and needed a letter of recommendation, which I was happy to provide.

Can you begin to sense the energy flowing though this experience?

Can you see the relationships blooming, the business benefits building like an avalanche rolling down a steep mountain?

And remember, it started with one stray tweet, "Go Steelers!"

It seems like a lot of *luck* was involved for all of this to happen, right?

Wrong. <u>This was not luck.</u> This exchange was enabled by the Tao, the secret sauce that experienced Twitter networkers and marketers sense but may not be able to name or explain. There is an underlying wisdom that created this success story and thousands of others like it.

Let's use this fun little story to explain this formula, The Tao of Twitter.

Tao Explained

I have studied, observed, and written about hundreds of different "success stories" through Twitter and the social web and they all have one common formula running through them. This is truly the path, the way, the Tao of Twitter.

Business benefits are created through three elements:

Targeted Connections
+
Meaningful Content
+
Authentic Helpfulness

Let's see how this worked in the real world.

Targeted Connections

No amount of work, time, or dedication to marketing and social media networking will work if you haven't surrounded yourself with people who might be interested in you and what you have to say.

So while it might seem like the Mark-Michelle-Trey story was random, the conditions were ripe for this connection because all three of us had systematically surrounded ourselves with people likely to want to know us, learn from us, and help us.

In the next chapter, we'll go through many ideas on how to create these conditions for yourself. Networking doesn't occur by chance in the traditional business world and it doesn't occur by chance alone on the social web either.

In the "Go Steelers" story, Michelle, Trey, and I had purposefully selected each other at some point in the past, even though we had no idea what, if anything, might happen in the future. That's the majestic random synergy of Twitter that I mentioned earlier.

Think about Twitter followers like atoms flying around inside of a chemist's test tube, bumping into each other randomly. Obviously the more atoms you have in the tube, the better your chances that a reaction will occur!

But every chemical reaction needs a catalyst, and on Twitter that catalyst is...

Meaningful Content

Content is the currency of the social web and sharing that content is the catalyst to new relationships and business benefits.

Let's look at the role of Meaningful Content in this story. What <u>was</u> the content that created these powerful connections?

Tweets – Our first connection came through my simple tweet about a football game. There's an important truth here. My tweet was not a PhD thesis, a white paper, or even a blog post. But it was meaningful to the person receiving it.

This is a lesson that is lost on many people trying to network on the social web. They have highly-engineered content aimed at certain buyer personas. And while there is value to this -- both in theory and practice -- networking and marketing on the social web isn't about Search Engine Optimization or keywords or B2B or B2C, it's all about *P2P – person to person connections.*

There is a high value for authenticity and being human on Twitter, a lesson I learned early on. Like a classic marketer, I wanted to "reach" my "targeted audience" with well-defined "messaging." But at some point, I relaxed and was just me. At that crossroad, a wonderful breakthrough occurred. Instead of trying to find my audience and customers, they found me. <u>Twitter is about content for humans, not search engines.</u>

Blogs – Blogs and Twitter fit like a hand in a glove. Some have likened Twitter to the trailer to the blog's movie.

No matter how you describe it, the tweets about my blog attracted Michelle's attention and it was this content -- highly meaningful to her as a fellow marketer – that created an incentive for her to take the next step in the relationship, to connect, and ask for help.

Likewise, her content definitely attracted my attention, too. Blogs can play an important role in this respect. Profiles, status updates, and resumes may *indicate* that you know your stuff but blogs *demonstrate* that you know it!

I also used my ability to create content on my blog to showcase Michelle and her formidable video talents.

Links – For the sake of brevity, I didn't get into the daily details of our Twitter relationship, but Michelle, Trey, and I stay in each other's orbits through interesting and helpful links we tweet each day. These tweets could link to articles, videos, photographs – just about any kind of content that would be interesting and useful.

Other kinds of content that served as catalysts for business benefits were Michelle's videos and Trey's podcasts.

And finally, none of this would have happened without...

Authentic Helpfulness

This third and final factor is the one that is most mis-used, misunderstood, and simply ignored by most folks using Twitter today. This is an extremely important and subtle difference between traditional sales/marketing and new media. I think it can be best illustrated through this question...

Do you believe that at any time in this evolving relationship my aim was to sell my professional services to Trey or Michelle?

I hope you replied "no"... and if you did you're on your way to understanding this very crucial and important aspect to the new media marketing mindset.

At least for the foreseeable future, there will be a place for cold-calling and the traditional sales function. When you schedule a call on a new client in many industries, they expect you to go through a tailored and well-rehearsed sales pitch.

But that simply doesn't work on the social web. People are sick of being sold to, marketed to, and tricked into clicking on links to unwanted products.

In an always-on, real-time, global world of business communications, the priority is on *human interaction* that leads to connections. Connections lead to awareness. Awareness leads to trust. Trust is the ultimate catalyst to business benefits.

I'm going to devote a chapter to each of these three integrated elements of The Tao of Twitter. None of them can succeed independently of the other.

Before we dive into these important concepts and learn some practical applications, let's take a closer look at what we're really after here.

Why are we doing this? What are the business benefits of Twitter?

Business Benefits of Twitter

In the case study I used to illustrate the Tao of Twitter, no direct sale was made and yet I believe you'll agree that the benefits were powerful and undeniable. They included:

- Michelle receiving feedback on her blog and videos
- A new HD video camera for Michelle
- A mentoring relationship for Michelle
- A new company video for my website
- Blog post content for Mark
- Podcast content for Trey
- Publicity for Michelle
- A customer for Trey
- Job advice for Michelle
- A marketing position for Trey
- Support on video technical problems for Mark

- Invitation to Paris party for Mark
- New international blogging connections for Mark
- A work visa recommendation for Michelle's friend
- And most important for all of us, friendships that will last throughout the years.

And all of this occurred within one year!

I'm spending time discussing the business benefits of Twitter because this is where most companies miss a big opportunity. They don't want to devote resources to an activity without a measurable return on investment.

And for many well-managed companies, this mindset has worked well in the past. But if you look at the list above and other potential benefits of Twitter such as:

- Competitive intelligence
- Market insight
- A new supplier or partner
- Publicity
- Brand awareness
- An idea
- New products
- And yes, even a potential customer

... most of these benefits are <u>intangible</u> and difficult to display in an Excel spreadsheet! So why keep trying to do it? Here's an example.

I once recognized somebody at a networking meeting from their Twitter picture. Because I had been following his "tweets," I knew that he had just started a new online business, he had two little boys, had recently vacationed in California, and was a baseball fanatic. I had never met him before in my life but when I introduced myself, he gave me a bear-hug and greeted me like a long-lost friend! Through my stream of information on Twitter, he felt he knew me too. We had formed a connection that led to friendship and trust.

The meeting was about to start and we didn't have time to chat, but we exchanged phone numbers and committed to meet for coffee to talk about ways we could work together. He eventually became one of my best customers.

Now, how many cold calls would you have to make to find a new business connection who greets you with a hug on the first meeting? I had effectively used Twitter to <u>pre-populate the business relationship!</u> And yes, it did eventually result in sales, but more important it resulted in a new business connection that can result in opportunities for years to come.

I'm an old-school data junkie. But as a small business owner, I don't find it necessary to formally calculate the ROI of Twitter (even though it may be possible) because the value I am receiving is instinctive and self-regulating. I have precious little time, so I better get something important out of Twitter if I am going to devote resources to it. Like any investment in time or money, if I don't realize a benefit, I will pull back.

It gets more difficult for a larger business conditioned to run on data and not the entrepreneurial instinct of doing something because you KNOW it works or because it "rocks." That simply doesn't fly in a boardroom. And yet spending time and money trying to quantify some of the intangible business benefits of Twitter can be a complete waste of time.

So how do you break the ice? When benefits are difficult to quantify, the best way to explain the value is often through a story.

For most experienced business people, hearing a compelling story of Twitter success can be just as effective as a pie chart. Once somebody understands how the networking operates and the RANGE of business benefits that exist beyond just money, it's easy to make the decision to give it a chance. And once they try it, they're usually hooked!

At least that's the way it has worked for me and many of my students and customers. Why keep fretting over measuring something that can't be easily measured? Just *show* them.

Another useful tactic is the pilot program. People get nervous about commitment. Ask your boss if you can test it for six months. Then week by week, pass along the stories as the tangible and intangible benefits accrue. Or, perhaps they won't. Then you can kill the thing gracefully and still get a good performance review!

I think if you follow the guidelines in this book, you WILL see the benefits. No matter your industry or specialty, whether you're a profit or non-profit, whether you work for a Fortune 500 of for yourself, Twitter can absolutely be applied to the business world.

But I still observe many companies stumbling around trying to calculate their return on investment while their competitors are establishing a social media foothold on a business communication platform that is:

An effective promotional tool[1] -- 79% of Twitter followers

---

[1] http://blog.cmbinfo.com/press-center-content/bid/46920/Consumers-En
gaged-Via-Social-Media-Are-More-Likely-To-Buy-Recommend

(versus 60% of Facebook fans) are more likely to recommend brands since becoming a fan or follower. 67% of Twitter followers (versus 51% of Facebook fans) are more likely to buy the brands they follow. Daily Twitter users are about three times as likely as Internet users on average to upload photos, four times as likely to blog, three times as likely to post ratings and reviews, and nearly six times as likely to upload articles.[2]

Lead Generator -- Marketing firm SocialTwist analyzed more than one million links on Facebook and Twitter. Facebook's shared links average only three clicks, while Twitter's tweets generate 19 clicks on average.[3] Another study showed that among many small and medium companies, Twitter users generated double the median monthly leads of non-Twitter users. That result held across company size.[4]

Customer Satisfier -- Service-related companies from appliance manufacturers to the local pizza joint are incorporating Twitter as a cost-effective and popular customer service connection.

Product Development Engine -- One software company developed an entirely new product line after learning from tweets that people were using their product in new ways. Interesting experiments are emerging to crowd-source innovation through Twitter.

Problem Solver -- David Sifry, CEO of Technorati was quoted[5] as saying he used Twitter as a sounding board. "I subscribe to lots of people who say interesting things, and I listen [and] read a lot.

---

[2] http://www.mediapost.com/publications/?fa=Articles.showArticle&art_aid=133837&nid=117809

[3] http://www.businessinsider.com/twitter-destroys-facebook-2010-12

[4] http://www.emarketer.com/Article.aspx?R=1007639

[5] http://images.businessweek.com/ss/08/09/0908_microblogceo/index.htm

I find that these people become a sounding board for ideas, and I learn a lot from them. When I post to Twitter, sometimes it's about interesting things I've seen or observed, and sometimes it's 'questions to the world'—where to find a good consultant for a particular niche specialty—or I ask questions that I can't find easy or reliable answers [to] just by searching Google or reference works."

Using Twitter as a Strategic Weapon

Here's an example of how I realized an exceptional and unexpected benefit from Twitter -- developing a PR strategy!

I have a "virtual" company. Well, it's a real company, but I don't have a building and employees and all that traditional stuff. I work with a posse of talented freelancers who might be spread out all over the country. So, I have the best of both worlds. Great company, great people, but no pressure about meeting payroll every month (except my own!).

Everything works great about this model except for one thing. You can't brainstorm by yourself.

This was the problem I was facing recently when I needed to come up with creative ideas to help a client company mark its 30th anniversary. I had some ideas, but I've been around long enough to know they weren't the BEST ideas. For that, I needed to put some minds together. But how? I was on a tight deadline and needed to write a proposal quickly.

I needed some smart friends that could help me think through this problem in a pinch. And then it dawned on me! That's exactly what I had on Twitter.

This is what the social web is all about — networking, sharing, helping, creating. So with literally no planning, I sent out one single tweet with an invitation for my Twitter tribe to join me on a web meeting at 4 p.m. that very day.

I was fortunate that seven people were able to join me on the spur of the moment, including one from Brazil and one from Spain Some I didn't know at all, others had become my friends over months of interaction on Twitter. All were enthusiastic, helpful and eager to try out this idea of mine!

I used an online service for the actual meeting interface and conference call. To start the meeting, I described the problem and said I was simply looking for a brainstorm of promotional options.

As the ideas were shared, I wrote them out on my shared computer screen so all participants could build on what was being said. At the end of 30 minutes, I had two pages filled with great ideas. Later that day I massaged the ideas into a proposal, presented it to company management and -- ta-da! -- they loved it! I had successfully "crowd-sourced" a brainstorming session!

There were unexpected side benefits, too:

- I explained to my client how I came up with the ideas, which further strengthened their interest and commitment to the social web.
- The people who connected on the call enjoyed the exercise and have reached out to stay connected between themselves.
- I had an idea that worked, it can be repeated, and now shared with you in a book!

Creating a New Product Line

One of the readers of my blog, Fara Hain, described how Twitter search helped her discover an entirely new market for her company's product:

"I admit my initial impression of Twitter was that it was pointless. But it didn't take too long to make me a believer because I saw first-hand how Twitter helped our company create an entirely new line of business.

"While working at Gizmoz (now digime), I was pulled into the world of Twitter by two friends who were early adopters. They encouraged me to try it out and I started by "listening" through a daily search for Gizmoz on the Twitter search box. I thought it would be interesting to see what, if anything, people were saying about us. I collated responses into a spreadsheet to see if I could find a theme or locate emerging influencers.

"I found that there was a group of people using my site in a completely different way than I had expected. Gizmoz is a B2C 3D animation company that had launched a web-based tool for teens to create greetings and videos using 3D avatars. On Twitter, our tool was being discussed with hashtags like #edtech.

"It turns out we were being discussed on the podium at a major education conference! To my surprise, teachers had been using Gizmoz in the classroom as an interactive tool for students to create presentations (science classes, social studies, even a kindergarten class!). We were blown away.

"By making some simple changes to our product, and asking teachers for their direct feedback, we were able to make Gizmoz more classroom-friendly. We added avatars like Albert Einstein and other historical figures and we started to be more aggressive about hiding public posts which featured less appropriate content.

"In our new marketing effort, we actively targeted teachers – who are, in fact, major viral influencers – one teacher influencing 30 students is a marketer's dream!

"It's doubtful that I would have ever discovered this amazing new market for our products without Twitter."

The Power of the Twitter Universe

One last potential business benefit you might not have considered: The power of the Twitter users to be advocates for your products and brands.

A study[6] found that consumers active on Twitter are three times more likely to impact a brand's online reputation through syndicated Tweets, blog posts, articles and product reviews than the average consumer!

The ExactTarget survey of more than 1,500 consumers concludes that Twitter has become the gathering place for content creators whose influence spills over into every other corner of the internet.

- Twitter users are the <u>most influential online consumers</u> — More than 70 percent publish blog posts at least monthly, 70 percent comment on blogs, 61 percent write at least one product review monthly and 61 percent comment on news sites.

---

[6] http://www.exacttarget.com/

- Daily Twitter users are six times more likely to publish articles, five times more likely to post blogs, seven times more likely to post to Wikis and three times more likely to post product reviews at least monthly compared to non-Twitter users.

- 11 percent of online consumers read Twitter updates, but do not have a Twitter account themselves!

- 20 percent of consumers indicate they have followed a brand on Twitter in order to interact with the company — more than email subscribers or Facebook fans.

... and that's why I've spent so much space discussing benefits. Can you really afford to miss out?

Balance. Common sense. Qualitative measures like stories. Don't let your company miss out on these benefits if traditional measurements don't fit any more, and for heaven's sake don't get caught in analysis paralysis because you can't determine the ROI. To realize these powerful benefits, you need to master the Tao of Twitter, so let's get to it, step-by-step, beginning with those all-important targeted connections.

Tao 1: Attracting Targeted Followers

Many social media pundits and purists would like to have you believe that the quality of your Twitter followers is more important than the quantity. These folks are either naive or liars. In fact, you absolutely need both quality AND quantity.

Attracting a critical mass of Twitter followers -- and by this I mean about 200 in most cases -- is critical as you start your journey for two reasons:

- First, if you have less than 200 people who are connecting with you, Twitter is going to be boring. And if it's boring, you're going to quit.

- Second, the more followers you have, the better the chance for a "Go Steelers moment." The more followers, the more potential interactions, the more interactions, the more opportunities to create business benefits. And we all LOVE those!

So I strongly recommend that you spend some time upfront

working on this critical aspect of your success – even as little as 20 minutes a day for a few weeks can get you started in the right direction.

"If you build it, they will come" makes a great movie line but a lousy Twitter strategy. There's no short-cut. The only viable and legitimate method to begin to attract targeted followers is to find them, follow them, and hope they follow you back. A rule of thumb is that about 70 percent of the people you follow will follow you back, but there are five simple ideas to tilt the follower-odds in your favor...

Five Set-up Basics

Twitter success starts with setting up your profile correctly. This can easily be accomplished under "settings."

When establishing your account here are some imperatives:

1) Always include a personal photo, preferably a friendly one. No picture = no followers. Trust me. Even if you are tweeting for a company, I would still recommend a photo of a person rather than a company logo in most cases. People relate to people, not logos. I'll cover this in more detail later on.

2) Include a link to your website. After all, you eventually want to drive people there, right? If you don't have a website, direct people to your LinkedIn profile or Facebook page.

3) Create a biography with your business interests that will help people find you in searches. Add some personality! Think about the keywords people would use to find you and your business. Although your bio isn't searchable on Twitter (yet) third party services can use it to help people find you.

4) Choose a short, easy to remember user name like Sally_R. A name like vls767p1 is counter-productive.

5) Even if nobody is following you yet, add a few tweets. People will usually check out your profile and what you have tweeted before deciding to follow you.

Ok, with these profile basics in place, let's start to discuss follower strategies.

Finding Followers

"Following" someone is the same thing as adding them as a Facebook friend, except that they don't see your updates unless they choose to follow you as well. Generally the best way to get followers is to add people based on your interests and business synergies.

Remember that it's not essential for somebody to follow you for you to still realize some business benefits. Twitter is a great learning tool so if a celebrity, author, industry leader, or professor doesn't follow you back, relax and just enjoy the information they provide.

Once you start following someone, their updates, or "Tweets," will appear in the "timeline" on your home page. The timeline is just a chronological record of what your followers are saying to you and the rest of the world.

By the way, if you're wondering why the system is limited to 140 characters per tweet, it's because Twitter was built to accommodate being updated from phones. The origin of the 140 character limit is based on the 160 character limit for SMS, which leaves some space for a name in addition to a 140 character message.

15 Ways to Attract Targeted Followers

The first quest of a new Twitter user is to add followers who are interested in the same topics as you. Twitter doesn't really get fun and useful until you have a couple hundred people in your "tribe."

Once you've exhausted your personal and professional contacts, where do you go from there? Generally, Twitter users follow a rule of reciprocity. If somebody follows you, it is polite to follow them back. Many people are amending this rule over time as the number of Twitter followers grows, but if somebody shares similar interests, they will probably follow you back – the rule of thumb is they reciprocate about 70 percent of the time. So a key idea as we get started is to follow people first, and they will probably follow you in return. Here are a few ideas to build that first targeted audience:

1) Start following people who you already know by looking for them on Twitter using the "Search box" at the top of your Twitter screen. This way you can find existing customers, contacts, friends and colleagues. Twitter People Search is a great *starting point* to find people that may already be on Twitter.

2) Once you are on Twitter for awhile, people will place you on public "lists." These are generally categorized by a special interest or geographic location. For example, I might be on lists for "marketing experts," "bloggers," or "business educators." If you dig into these lists you will find similar people to follow. Lists are important for many reasons that we'll cover later.

3) Look for lists that follow your key stakeholders. For example, if you find a competitor that keeps lists, you might want to check it out and "steal" their followers. All of these lists are

public so there are no ethical problems with this at all.

4) Probably my favorite place to find targeted followers for my clients and students is Twellow.com. This useful little site is kind of like the yellow pages for Twitter. Simply sign in for free with your Twitter information and you're ready to find and follow targeted users. It does not have a complete list of all Twitter users, but it's a pretty good start. Twellow has four useful features:

   a. It has an exhaustive directory of Twitter members by every category, industry and interest imaginable. Want to find civil engineers? Knitters? Dog lovers? They're all here. Results are displayed from the person with the most users to the least.

   b. You can also see Twitter users by city, very useful if you only serve a special market.

   c. You can search for people by interest AND region.

   d. You can add yourself to up to 10 special interest categories to make it easy for people to find you.

5) Do a Twitter search by your business interests and follow those who pop up. They will likely look at your profile and become one of your followers. For example, if you are in construction, try searching by:

#construction
#building
#architecture
#remodeling

6) Watch who your followers are recommending and tweeting. Click on their name and see if you want to follow them. In turn, they will probably follow you. Follow Friday (covered below) is a great way to find people who might interest you.

7) Connect with contacts on Facebook, LinkedIn and other social media platforms. For example, most LinkedIn accounts now include a Twitter handle. This is a great way of finding people in your industry to follow!

8) Go to TwitterGrader.com. You can find the top Twitter users in a city.

9) Search www.listorious.com for Twitter users by hundreds of interest categories. A gold mine. Curating relevant, targeted lists is a big deal.

10) Some Twitter applications, like Tweetie, LocalChirps and TwitterLocal let you search posts and tweeters near you. Check the web site Happn.in to see the most discussed topics in your area.

11) Attend Twitter chats based on your industry/interests and follow them. There is more information on chats in the "Advanced" section of this document. These chats are a great way to find and meet people with similar interests.

12) Another cool third party application is www.wefollow.com. The user- generated directory has lists of people who associate themselves with particular keywords and interests.

13) Mr. Tweet is another popular recommendation engine that is updated daily.

14) Use Twitter's standard "Suggestions for You" function on

every home page. The algorithm in this feature suggests people you don't currently follow who you may find interesting. The suggestions are based on several factors, including people you follow and the people they follow. You'll see these suggestions on Twitter.com and the Find People section. If you like a suggestion, click "follow," if you don't, click "hide," and they won't suggest that user again.

15) "Similar to you" is another Twitter suggestion service right on your home page. They have an uncanny ability to find people who you will probably like!

Follower Strategies

Once you begin collecting followers, people will also start finding you. It can be unsettling when people from all over the world start showing up in your list of followers. What do you do about these people?

You'll see two general strategies when it comes to decisions about following people back. There is one group of "celebrities" who might have 50,000 followers but only follow a few hundred back. Comedian and TV personality Conan O'Brien famously follows only one person!

But if you're not a celebrity (and I'm pretty sure you're not) it's usually a good idea to give people the benefit of the doubt and follow them back. Here's the rule of creating relationships and business benefits through Twitter: *You just never know.*

You never know who will connect with you, you never know how they will connect with you, and you never know where it will lead (Go Steelers!).

Having said that, there is a certain element of undesirables who try to corrupt the conversation by spamming. Twitter does a fairly good job culling these folks but they need our help too. I go the extra step and "block" people who do not seem to be real people for four reasons:

1) Your list of followers is public information and reflects on you in some small way. I want an audience to be proud of. This probably sounds old-fashioned but I don't want to do anything in my life that I wouldn't be proud to disclose to my children. And if they examined my Twitter audience, I would not want them to see a bunch of nymphs peddling their videos. Anybody can see who you're following. What does your audience say about you?

2) I want to protect my followers. If I block the spamaholics I keep them from my tweets and I keep them, in a small way, from my friends. I see so many of these folks who copy "Follow Friday" lists trying to lure followers in a sneaky way.

3) Because I just do not want to play that game. I'm not going to be passive and imply that what they're doing is OK.

4) Blocking spammers sends a message and that's important. But I increasingly believe that having a **quality list of followers** who actually exist and care about you is going to make a difference in social influence scoring models such as Klout. These systems are becoming important business tools.

How Many Followers is Enough?

The answer depends entirely on your business strategy. As I said, you need a couple hundred folks for Twitter to start to get interesting, but remember that you are trying to build a **relevant** and **targeted** community. The more people who follow you, the less real interaction you will have with them so choose your "tweeps" carefully.

Let's say you are trying to connect to people who enjoy single malt Scotch in a limited geographic area. A few hundred followers may be all you need. In my business, I can sell my marketing consulting services literally anywhere in the world, so my potential audience is in the hundreds of thousands of people.

Once you get over a few hundred followers, you may need a little help keeping up, and that topic is covered in the "Advanced" section at the end.

A Word About Buying Twitter Followers

There simply is no shortcut to developing an effective, targeted tribe. I recently received this tweet:

"Thanks for the follow. I'm gaining daily new targeted followers with www.wyz.com. It's the company everyone uses. Let me know."

While that might sound like a great idea, it's a scam called GFF of Get Followers Fast. No knowledgeable Twitter user would use these services. Unfortunately where corruption can occur, corruption WILL occur and Twitter is no different. There is a cottage industry dedicated to building accounts of blank followers and then selling them for instant "credibility" to unsuspecting buyers.

I had a friend call me up and tell me he had just bought a Twitter account and had inherited 6,000 followers. "Now, what do I do next?" he asked.

My reply: "Start over."

There are plenty of scams out there. Avoid them all. Work it the way I've described here and you WILL create business benefits!

Tao 2: Providing Meaningful Content

When I started using Twitter I was clueless and frustrated. Sound familiar?

One of the lessons I learned on the path toward Twitter Tao was the power of content -- the currency of the social web.

Eager to learn all I could, I was a voracious consumer of free webinars. One session sponsored by the American Marketing Association featured a young entrepreneur named Nathan Egan (@nathanegan) a former LinkedIn executive who had formed a company called Freesource.

His concept was very interesting -- harnessing the power of free web resources to run your company and sales departments more cost-effectively. He hypothesized that the time was coming when you could even run an entire company off of free software and applications.

Nathan seemed like a bright guy and at the end of the webinar, he invited the participants to follow him on Twitter and LinkedIn, so I did.

Through our random posts on Twitter, we began to get to know each other. I was interested in the progress of his company and I apparently appeared on Nathan's radar too as he began reading my blog, {grow}.

One day, out of the blue, I received a phone call from Nathan. I had just posted a new article that had really resonated with him. "Do you have time to talk for a few minutes?" he asked. "What you wrote reflects my thinking on some things and I have never really found anybody who understood this topic this way."

We hit it off and ended up conversing for more than an hour!

Over the next few months, we continued to support each other and share ideas for our respective businesses.

Nathan assembled a great team and Freesource grew quickly as businesses sought the company's advice on using the social web to make their businesses more productive and efficient. As the client base grew, he needed a wide variety of resources to support projects, and, since I can do a wide variety of things, I seemed to fit the bill! Nathan began sending me paid assignments to fill in the many white spaces of a start-up company.

I loved the work because our views on business and marketing were aligned and I absolutely bought into his vision of how the new media could work for a corporation. As Nathan's trust in me grew, he provided more important, strategic assignments with his Fortune 500 clients.

Freesource quickly became one of the most respected social media marketing agencies in the country. Nathan no longer had time to work on the critical marketing functions of his company and asked me if I could help out on a higher level. At one point, I agreed to act as Chief Marketing Officer on a part-time basis and help him through this exciting growth phase.

I've continued to work with Nathan and he is one of my most important and cherished customers.

As you see from this example, Nathan and I had done a good job of surrounding ourselves with potential business connections – the first step in the Tao of Twitter -- but the synergy would not have occurred without some kind of <u>content</u> to grab our attention. Simply hanging out on Twitter or passively observing tweets from others was not going to do it. The catalyst for this connection -- and every connection -- is CONTENT.

What was the content that enabled these business benefits?

- The webinar first introduced Nathan to a group of relevant and targeted people.
- We both tweeted interesting marketing links, ideas and observations on a regular basis that kept us on each other's radar screen. We were PRESENT on Twitter!
- My blog posts finally served as a catalyst for conversation.

Let's explore this idea of providing consistent, compelling content to energize our new Twitter connections.

A Twitter Content Strategy

The key to turning a faceless follower into a real business relationship is to have a presence on the social web with relevant and interesting content. When I discussed the strategy of building targeted followers, this covered the WHO of tweeting. Now, we're going to cover the HOW, WHAT and WHEN.

The type of messages you send out will ultimately determine your success and effectiveness on Twitter. If you are interesting, funny, and help people with useful information, your followers will be drawn to you and also recommend others to follow you.

If you've never tweeted before, getting started can be difficult, maybe even paralyzing! Sometimes you just get stuck on what to do or say. If you're a newcomer in that category, you might need...

A Beginner's Twitter Regimen

Once you get into the tweeting rhythm, it's a lot of fun, but like anything, it can be awkward at first. Here are some ideas to help you become a Twitter pro in less than 15 minutes a day.

1) Try tweeting three times a day, at different times of the day. To start, tweet about a) some interesting non-work-related information you saw, heard or read; b) some news related to your business, market, or industry and c) your opinion on something going on in the news or something funny.

2) Check and respond to tweets that mention you and Direct Messages every time you log on.

3) Spend some time reading tweets from the people you follow. Re-tweet somebody at least once a day, and preferably more. Select a very interesting post from somebody and pass it along to others. Remember to use this format: RT @*follower name* message.

4) If it's Friday, tweet a Follow Friday[7] message for your favorite

---

[7] If you're completely new to Twitter and unfamiliar with terms such as "direct message" or "Follow Friday" don't worry! These are explained in the strategy section under the Language of Twitter.

friends. It might go like this: #FF to these awesome folks: *@followername1 @followername2 @followername3*

When to Tweet

Tweet in Peak Times, basically during the day throughout the work week. If you want to account for time differences in North America, aim for morning to early afternoon. If your business has international customers, think about the effectiveness of tweeting at different times of the day. Your messages will be more effective if you leave time between your tweets – at least 30 minutes and preferably an hour.

Tweet Regularly. Tweet often, but *only if you have something of value to say.* You should aim for at least a few tweets a day. **Do not have somebody tweet for you** - your followers will eventually figure it out and un-follow you. Remember, this is about building human, P2P connections.

Scheduling Tweets – Some people like to schedule their tweets to appear at regular intervals even when they're not at the keyboard. There can be valid business reasons for this. An example would be my friend Aaron Lee (@askaaronlee). Aaron lives and studies in Malaysia but is trying to build a following of business leaders in America. Unless he stays up all night, he probably doesn't have a choice but to schedule his tweets and hope to form new connections in other time zones. He also does an exceptional job following up with people wherever they may be in the world.

However, under normal conditions, Twitter is about engaging, not broadcasting, so it probably does not make sense to just broadcast on a regular schedule.

What to Tweet

Here is the best, simplest advice I can provide – tweet about what interests you. Although I am a marketing professional and enjoy communicating about that topic, I also love (and tweet about) sports, travel, art, technology, history, science, and many other subjects. I think that helps keep it real and human.

One of the common complaints about Twitter is "I'm not interested in what you had for dinner." Point taken. Still, it is only human – and I think beneficial – to occasionally talk about human stuff – even eating – once in awhile, especially as it relates to value-added information like a new restaurant or brand you're trying out.

The second most important advice I can provide is to get in a regular habit of sharing. You're already reading much of the day, right? Nearly every newspaper, magazine, blog, and video service allows you to share the content by clicking a tweet button right on their page. When you read something you like, tweet it.

Here's a little system that works for me. When I exercise in the morning, I read an electronic copy of the New York Times. If I see a particularly fascinating article about a new social media platform for example, with a push of a button I can "tweet" this article effortlessly to my audience. I have just provided great, interesting content with literally no effort ... even while I'm doing something else. Mobile devices can also help you keep on top of content and connecting during downtimes.

Finding interesting content is important to attracting and retaining followers. Be sure to mine content from all the sources you might connect with during the day...

- Linking to your blog and other blogs is an obvious source of rich and relevant content.
- When you tweet something that another person has contributed, that is called a re-tweet or an "RT." RTs have three

important benefits.

1. It takes the burden of providing all of the content off of you.
2. It is a compliment and form of engagement with the person who originated the content.
3. It puts you on the radar screen of the person you tweeted. Really want to get somebody to follow you? Tweet their content a few times and see what happens!

- Link to comments you create on LinkedIn, Facebook, and other platforms.
- Provide human content. Tell a little about yourself along the way. That's interesting too... to a point!
- Tweet out an opinion about a special event, something in the news, a development in your company or community.
- Leverage your other online content. If you have something of value to offer online, like a blog, white paper, or a website, share updates and new posts that you have written.
- Share something human. Did your baby take a first step? Did you close a big deal? Are you grateful for something today? Share it!

Snip, Snip, Snip

A URL is the unique name used to identify a website. In fact every piece of content on the web – a post, a video, a photo – has its own descriptor.

Problem is, most of these names are long – quite the problem if you are limited to 140 characters to begin with on a Twitter message! Fortunately some smart people solved the problem with an application called a URL shortener or "snipper."

When you hit a "tweet button" on an article, the URL is usually shortened automatically. But if you need to shorten a website name, this is easily done with an application such as bit.ly (no "www" just bit.ly). In addition to being a handy little snipper, bit.ly allows you to track how many people actually clicked on your link. This can be very useful marketing information if you are trying to determine interest in an announcement, testing different times or methods of tweeting, or if you want to track promotions.

OK, you are one amazing content provider now. But there's still one important aspect of the Tao of Twitter left...
Authentic Helpfulness.

Tao 3: Offering Authentic Helpfulness

When somebody does something great -- an interesting blog post, an exceptional insight, a helpful solution -- I try to make an effort to compliment them publicly on Twitter. Usually I will just tweet something like "@jfloyd helped me with a problem today. You should definitely follow Jeremy!"

One day I received a tweet from a stranger asking "We follow each other. Why don't you ever recommend ME?"

My response was: "Because I don't know who you are! Let's change that."

It turns out this stranger was a bright young man named Aaron Killian. I had met him briefly at a speech I gave but didn't know his name and we had never connected. Since he lived nearby, I invited him to lunch.

When we met, I discovered that Aaron is a marketing professional with a local United Way. He told me how many non-profits were struggling in the tough economy, and that meant a lot of needy people were suffering, too. It prompted an idea on how we might work together.

"I've long thought that charities could benefit from using social media tools," I said. "After all, who better needs to get more out of their marketing dollars? I've been thinking about an idea to give back to the community. What if I volunteered my time to do a workshop for some of the area non-profits?"

Of course Aaron was interested in the possibilities and after some discussions with his president and CEO, we arrived on a concept. I committed to volunteering a full-day of social media training to as many people as they could fit in their conference center.

As the day of the seminar grew closer, it occurred to me that this could be an opportunity to create some video content for my business. When I give speeches, it can be difficult and costly to arrange for professional video services. Under controlled conditions in my hometown, this would really save me some time and money. I asked Aaron if we could video the session and he readily agreed. We were able to create two videos which are on my website today promoting my availability as a business conference speaker and trainer.

A few days before the event, I tweeted that I was preparing my materials for a seminar for local non-profits. This information was picked up by a Twitter friend, Tearsa Smith, an anchor for the local TV station. She invited Aaron to a live television appearance on her morning show to promote the event. Twitter is an important source of information and leads for journalists!

The United Way seminar went off without a hitch but Aaron had to deliver some bad news during the meeting. A local center focused on providing support to area non-profits announced they would be closing within the next two months. It appeared that the need to use Twitter and other social media tools was more important than ever!

The participants were so enthusiastic about my workshop that they proposed meeting every quarter to discuss social media marketing issues. By meeting regularly they could exchange best practices and look for ways to learn together.

Several of the people decided they loved my ideas so much they wanted to sign up for my college course on social media marketing for business. Not only did they attend, but they also referred others who have now become my students, my friends, and in one case, a new customer!

And oh yes -- Aaron finally got his complimentary tweet!

So now let's look at the final aspect of the Tao of Twitter -- Authentic Helpfulness. How did it show up in this case study?

- The fact that I was routinely complimenting and supporting other people got Aaron's attention. It made an impact on him, and he wanted to be included.
- We both wanted to meet to get to know each other better.
- By spending the time to meet him for lunch, I was turning an online relationship into an offline relationship. This is a very important part of crystallizing relationships.
- I volunteered my time for the seminar.
- Aaron allowed me to have a video professional record the session to benefit my business.
- I subsequently offered advice and support to participants, some of whom later became my students.

There was a theme of helpfulness throughout this story. It was real. I wasn't looking to sell anything to anybody. Aaron wasn't looking to game me -- we were authentically supporting each other.

A Mindset of Helpfulness

I find many of the social media axioms to be dumb ("it's all about the conversation"... gag me) but here is one that is very useful: Think of the social web as a dinner party. If somebody only talks about themselves, their business and how great they are, you're going to want to get away fast! But if a person shows genuine interest in you, and offers help without regard for their own personal benefit, you will like that person and connect with them.

Like any business relationship, friendships on the social web are built on trust and that must be earned.

This is the area where most people fail on Twitter because you can't fake authenticity. If you're only out there to sell, sell, sell, people will sniff you out pretty quickly. Here are some ways to demonstrate true helpfulness to others and engage in a way that *builds relationships:*

- People throw questions out there all the time. Answer them or refer them to somebody who can.

- Build your own tribe. Reach out to the real people on Twitter, don't just kiss up to the most influential folks. Are those folks really going to deliver business benefits to you?

- Read people's profiles. Visit their websites, read their blogs and comment. You can almost always find something in common with them and this shows you are genuinely interested. And you should be!

- Nothing says I love you like a re-tweet now and then.

- Check your @ mentions frequently. Make sure you know who is mentioning you and try to respond to them or acknowledge them promptly.

- Show gratitude. If someone's helped you out, be sure to thank them publicly.

- Be genuine. Stay honest and let people see your personality.

- Take extended or private conversations to DM.

- Use every opportunity to extend the conversation and the relationship by taking it offline. Connect in a deeper way through email, a phone call, or a live meeting.

Being genuine and helpful sounds so easy doesn't it? But of the three aspects of the Tao of Twitter, this is the one that is most easily over-looked and abused by business professionals trying to fit the old "broadcast" mode of communicating into this new format.

Now that we've walked through the fundamental aspects of the Tao of Twitter, let's look at putting it into action!

Immersion

If you follow the path of Targeted Connections, Meaningful Content and Authentic Helpfulness, you will have an enormous competitive advantage over those who might take months or years to understand these lessons -- if they ever learn them at all.

But even with this knowledge, Twitter can be daunting. It has its own language and vibe. People toss around hashtags and Twitter chats and so many other quirky acronyms that it can make your head spin.

In this chapter I'm going to cover some ideas to help you get on the fast-track, speed your learning curve, and gain a competitive edge in the Twitter Universe! Let's cover:

- The Language of Twitter
- Getting the most from your tweets
- Corrective actions if you fall off track

Let's cut through the clutter one step at a time beginning with...

The Language of Twitter

Learning some of the common terms and acronyms is one of the most important things you can do to put yourself at ease. If you're a Twitter pro, you'll be familiar with the ideas in this section but if you're new this is going to help a lot! Here are a few of the most common terms and designations you will encounter:

@ **reply** -- The @ sign is used to indicate that you are replying to a specific username. For example, if your friend Jim Smith tweets a question asking about the best place to buy a Jeep, you will reply with @JimSmith (or whatever the handle is) "I have one for sale, come on over." Remember that when you use @reply it is visible to everyone - **for private communications use a direct message.**

Avatar -- The personal image uploaded to your Twitter profile in the Settings tab of your account.

Blocking -- The act of blocking keeps a particular Twitter user name from following you and your tweets. You block someone by clicking on their profile and choosing "Block" in the settings.

Block and Report -- Twitter also gives you the opportunity to block somebody and if you think they are doing something offensive or illegal you can also "report" them to the service. After a few reports like this, they can be suspended from Twitter.

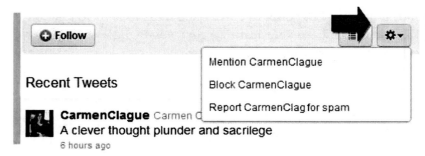

On a profile, the ability to "block" or "report" is found by clicking the little settings wheel.

Direct Messages, or DM -- Twitter equivalent to e-mail. You may only send direct messages to those you follow and who are also following you. To do so, click on "Message" on their profile and type out your message, again only up to 140 characters.

Feed -- Your posts on Twitter are commonly referred to as your "Twitter feed" or "timeline."

Fail Whale -- When Twitter is over-capacity and unavailable, the following cartoon will appear. So when Twitter is having technical problems, "whale" jokes are common.

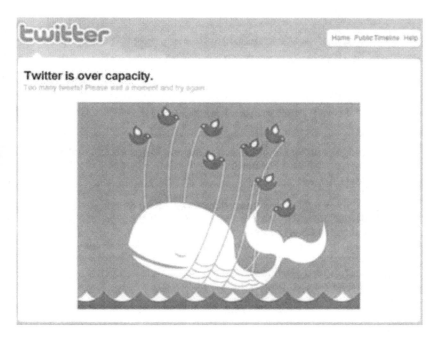

Favorites – Hover over any tweet in your stream and you will have the option to reply, re-tweet or favorite, which has a symbol of a star. If you click the star, this will save your Tweet under "favorites" on your home page. This is a handy tool if you want to come back to something at a later time.

Follow -- To follow someone on Twitter means to subscribe to their Tweets or updates on the site

Follow Friday or #FF -- It is a tradition to recommend your favorite followers every Friday. This is a polite way of thanking people who have done a good job or did something special to help you during the week. A typical format might be: #FF @*user1* @*user2* @*user3*

Hashtags -- Hashtags are optional but useful for denoting groups of tweets to follow. There are four primary uses for the hashtag groupings:

1) Discussions -- Some people will designate a hashtag to group all messages from an extended conversation. For example, try doing a search for #blogchat or #journchat in the Twitter search box. You'll find all comments on a certain topic. Here's an example of such a search:

loisgeller If you want to learn some new things about blogging, go to #blogchat **next Sunday night.**
about 1 hour ago via TweetDeck

ahynes1 @alisonlaw Thanks for RTing Music Mondays – Blog Mentor, Randy Burns: http://ad.vu/uich **You question on** #blogchat **last night was important**
about 2 hours ago via web from Westville, New Haven in reply to alisonlaw

searchguru @blogworld was a discussion in #blogchat **about Wordpress.com deleting my blogs.**
about 2 hours ago via TweetDeck in reply to blogworld

MackCollier @jenniesjursen @mikestenger Point I was trying to illustrate to #blogchat **participants was that interacting w others here drives traffic**
about 2 hours ago via TweetDeck

2) Topical groupings. If you have a comment you want to show up in a Twitter search, designate it with a hashtag. In this example, the author is indicating that the topic of his tweet is "social media." Anyone doing a search for this topic on Twitter would find his tweet.

joltsocialmedia Grandma
Interviews Brett Greene
http://bit.ly/9RAXzR #socialmedia
28m ago via twitterfeed | Twitter

3) Trending topics. If you want your tweet to reference a certain news or community event, hashtags can be very useful. For example, during a crisis like the flood in Nashville, citizens could follow news and emergency instructions by simply following #nashvilleflood on their Twitter search.

4) Silliness. People use whimsical hashtags just for fun:

KristenDaukas And now, for my
2,000th tweet, I want to say thanks
to all those that I tweet with & learn
from on a daily basis. You guys
rock. #gratitude
4m ago via HootSuite | Twitter

Locking -- You can "lock" your profile so that only friends can see your updates by scrolling down to the bottom of your "Settings" tab on the Twitter website and clicking the box beside "Protect My Updates."

This may **deprive you of followers** who would have otherwise followed you based on keywords in your posts and isn't advised for general use. After all, you're trying to network, right? Since you're reading this book to build business connections, I would strongly recommend that you keep your Twitter feed open and available to anyone who wants to interact with you.

What's happening?

[   ]

Timeline **@Mentions** Retweets ▾   Searches ▾   Lists ▾

Mentions -- Any time somebody uses the @ symbol with your Twitter name (also called handle), it will show up in your list of "mentions." This function is extremely important to monitor every day to see who is mentioning you in their tweets. Look for opportunities to engage and help people who are mentioning you.

Promoted Tweets -- Twitter is finding innovative ways to capitalize on its popularity and monetize its service without impeding users. One way they are doing this is by allowing brands to sponsor tweets and trending topics. Any tweet or promotion is supposed to be clearly marked as advertising or "promoted"

RT/Retweeting -- RT stands for re-tweet, meaning a "re-sent" message from someone else's Twitter post. If you see RT, this means it is not the sender's original content -- it came from the person listed after the RT designation. Another way to credit people for content or a link is to put via @username at the end of the tweet. There are many variations on this theme but the main point is, it's polite -- and good business -- to credit others for what you're doing.

Search -- Is located at the top of your Twitter home page. This is a powerful tool for finding people, links and the latest real-time news.

Trends or Trending Topics -- Located in the right hand column of your Twitter home page, this list indicates the most popular topics in real-time. This is an effective and entertaining way to see what people are saying about a subject in the moment, anywhere in the world. You will see tweets from anybody tweeting on a topic, not just your followers.

Tweeps/Tweeples -- A cluster of friends on Twitter. Frequently used to address all of your followers at once, e.g."Morning, Tweeples!" The Twitter World will try to force any kind of descriptive word into a format that begins with "Tw" unfortunately. Another common example is the...

Tweet-up -- Twitter folks are very loyal to each other and they love to meet in real life (IRL) at social gatherings called Tweet-ups. Tweet-ups may be formally scheduled as part of a meeting or conference or happen on the spur of the moment. The social side of social media! They can be great networking events.

Making the Most of Your Tweets

My friend Dr. Ben Hanna led an extensive statistical study to discover the optimal tweeting strategy. Here are four key findings to get the best results from your tweets.[8]

Tweet Quality Versus Tweet Quantity -- The study looked at the relevant importance of tweeting only when you had something really interesting to pass along (quality focus) vs. tweeting more frequently to make sure some content was in front of followers more often (quantity focus) for building a Twitter following. The study showed tweet quality is MUCH more important than quantity: the higher the average number of clicks per tweet with a trackable link in a given week, the higher the follower growth (controlling for total number of followers). This said, you still have to be in the game – average tweets-per-day over this period ranged from 2.9 to 11.0.

---

[8] http://www.businessesgrow.com/2009/07/13/twitter-for-business-four-breakthrough-insights/

The First Words Are Critical -- At 140 characters max, tweets are like headlines and people scan through them quickly. If you want to catch someone's eye, think like a headline writer and make sure the main topic keywords or a number/statistic are found in the first three to five words. The results also recommended against using the standard retweet style (e.g., "RT @ markwschaefer: ..." to start the tweet), instead shift attribution to the end of the tweet (e.g., "... via @markwschaefer").

The Average Lifespan of a Tweet -- If you measure the lifespan of a tweet by the number of days on which it receives at least one click from a Twitter user, then business tweets don't live very long. On average, tweets with a clickable link received at least one click on four separate days with a range of one day (not a very popular tweet) to 23 days (very popular content).

The Optimal Time Between Tweets -- In a study examining the number of clicks on business-related tweets, the optimal space between business tweets to attract the most clicks is either 31-60 minutes or 2-3 hours. Tightly packed tweets just don't appear to attract as much attention as tweets with more space between them. The cause of the dip in click activity for tweets between 61 and 120 minutes is uncertain.

If you get off track

Research shows 60 percent of those who try Twitter quit in the first week. Hey, I was one of them! It can be an incredibly frustrating experience, especially if you're trying to build momentum in a corporate environment. If you start spinning your wheels, here are a few strategies to get back on track.

Be Tenacious -- Twitter is a viable business communication channel, end of story. "From what I've determined in our research, Twitter has a role as a business communication channel for most companies," Dr. Hanna said "If you've already tried Twitter for your organization and struggled to make it work, it's most likely because the social media rules for your industry and customers are still being written. Don't give up."

Twitter as Mass Communication -- Maybe you feel like you're not connecting with followers like you should. Maybe it's time to review your fundamental strategy. Conventional wisdom among many Twitter-advocates is that you are building a "community." Certainly that can be true on a personal level, but necessarily for all businesses, according to Dr. Hanna.

"If you plan to use Twitter for business, and you have more than a few hundred prospects/customers/influencers combined, you're kidding yourself if you think interpersonal norms can govern how you use Twitter or other social media for your business," he said. "Why? Because Twitter is incredibly inefficient for forming inter-personal relationships on that scale. For the vast majority of businesses out there, mass communication is the model you should follow as you plan your Twitter strategy."

Is Anybody Home? -- If you are using the tools I've described to identify your list of meaningful connections and still can't find potential customers, maybe you need to review your strategy and underlying assumptions. Are your customers using social media? Is so, which ones? If not, are you in a position to lead and estab-lish a point of competitive differentiation? The nature of business communications is changing so rapidly, don't assume you really know your customers right now, especially if you don't see them often!

Focus on Quality -- You already know that tweeting interesting things has a much bigger, positive influence on follower growth rate than tweet volume. This holds true for businesses too. Blanketing your followers with tweets doesn't work any better than blanketing the media with press releases about non-issues or hammering a direct mail list with irrelevant offers. Here's a best practice idea for businesses -- Remember our little snipping tool friend bit.ly? Well, this application will show you how many people are clicking on your links, essentially "grading" your effectiveness. Experiment to find content and sources your customers like best.

Tao Times Two -- I've taught social media marketing classes to hundreds of business people and sometimes it just doesn't "take" the first time. Maybe the timing wasn't right. Or, they had other priorities at the time. Maybe the incentive didn't seem to be enough to be committed. Perhaps the first go-around of infor- mation was just too overwhelming. But usually everyone comes around. If you find yourself lagging behind, scan this book again, especially the first few chapters explaining Connections + Content + Helpfulness and the business benefits.

Be patient -- It might take months or even longer to realize business benefits from Twitter, depending on your devotion to the channel. In any event, it does take time and that fact doesn't go down easy for many impatient business owners. Follow the Tao of Twitter. It will happen.

Twitter Lists -- The Key to Sanity

Once you get more than a few hundred followers you're going to need some help. Twitter Lists will help keep you organized and tuned-in.

As you get into the flow of Twitter, you'll probably find yourself naturally grouping people in your mind. Customers. Competitors. My online friends. People I admire.

Twitter Lists allows you to organize the Twitter stream so you can make sense of what might seem like a wall of noise.

By clicking on the word "LISTS" in the right column of your Twitter page, you can build specific categories of followers such as "customers" or "thought leaders" or "friends" to make it easy to monitor the tweets from smaller groups of people who are impor-tant to you. You can make the Lists public for the world to see, or keep them private.

If you see lists from others that you like, you can "follow" this entire list. Likewise, others can follow your Lists. Some people are even making a business out of curating important and popular lists.

Eventually, you'll probably want to export your Twitter Lists to a third-party application called a "listening deck." More on that later.

So Lists are very important as a personal productivity tool but they are also important to businesses in many ways. I've already discussed their crucial role in finding targeted followers. Here are some additional ideas to leverage your public lists in creative ways:[9]

<u>Share your Lists on other platforms</u> -- Most people share their lists within Twitter. But don't stop there. Plan on sharing the links to your lists on your website or blog. Lists will be accessed via a URL like this: http://twitter.com/user_name/list_name. To promote the list on your website, you'll just add a link with the URL. Why not share them on Facebook, in email, and through your newsletter?

<u>Include yourself in your Lists</u> -- Since people can subscribe to your Lists, be sure to include yourself so they can see your tweets. As people follow these lists, they will following you, too.

<u>Name your Lists well</u> -- You'll give your Lists names, and those names will be part of the URL. Choose a name that is enticing and accurate such as "my favorite bloggers" or "metals industry experts."

<u>Create Lists helpful to your target audience</u> -- Think of Lists as

---

[9] Some of these ideas came from my friend, entrepreneur and blogger Neicole Crepeau: http://nmc.itdevworks.com/index.php/2009/10/5-clever-uses-for-lists/

a marketing tool. Ask yourself these questions (bloggers, replace "customer" with "audience"):

- Who are my target customers?
- Do they fall into distinct segments with different needs or interests? If so, define each customer segment.
- What are their goals, as they relate to my area of business?
- What kind of information helps them reach those goals?
- What kind of information is this type of customer generally interested in?
- Who on Twitter regularly tweets that kind of information?
- What Twitter resources can be valuable to this customer segment, given their goals?

Now, using the answers to that last question, create one or more Lists for each customer segment, designed to meet their goals. For example, let's say you're a realtor. You'd like to attract potential home buyers in the Chicago area. You might decide that the key customers you want to attract are: first-time home buyers and people thinking of selling. You come up with this list of information goals for first-time buyers:

- Information about the home-buying process
- Information about mortgage types, qualifying, and so on
- Tips for home-shopping
- Information about what to look for in walk-throughs, inspections, etc.
- How to decide what you want in a house
- Information about neighborhoods, amenities, schools, etc.
- Real estate market and interest rate trends

Based on this List, you're able to find several bloggers and home magazines on Twitter that tweet about home buying, loan types, the home buying process, etc. You find some good Twitter sources for mortgage and interest rate information. You find several Twitterers who tweet about Chicago neighborhood statistics or tweet links to articles and blog posts about neighborhoods, and so on. And you add all of these sources, and yourself of course, to create your Chicago First-Time Home Buyer List.

Remember, these Lists can also be followed by competitors! Be aware of the competitive environment.

<u>Use Lists to create mini-communities</u> -- Let's say you blog about parenthood, or you're a retailer that sells products for new and expecting parents. *Why not build a community that also aligns with your business needs?*

Create a list for expectant parents on Twitter. Make the initial list from whomever you know is expecting, then invite others to join your list. Spread your invitation far and wide on Twitter, your site, Facebook, etc. Expectant parents can send a message to you to get added to the list. Ask the List members to nominate other expectant parents on Twitter. Keep spreading the word until you hit the 500 List member limit.

Now, you've created a mini-community consisting of your target market. It's a great resource for the List members and provides a real service to them. It's a place they can go to view the tweets of other expectant parents, kind of like a chat room. In the process, you've met a whole bunch of new potential customers that you can now get to know and share your products with.

Well, by now I hope you're starting to get a little more comfortable and confident in the language and workings of the Twitter platform. And of course you're constantly working on your Tao: connections, content and helpfulness. Now, let's see how these ideas can be applied for specific business marketing initiatives.

16 Ideas to Toast Your Competition

Let's start putting some of these ideas to practical use for your business or organization. In fact, Twitter can be a powerful competitive advantage for many people!

Just because we're talking about marketing and competition, don't think I'm going to let you forget the "social" part of social media. Whether you work at a small business, a giant corporation, or a non-profit, I'd like you to take a post-it note and put this on your computer:

Social media is P2P

Person to person. This is the heart of our Tao, isn't it?
If you take one thing from this book -- and it is the one thing most businesses disregard -- remember that you are connecting to real people, not avatars. Business is built on relationships and you are only working toward that end if you keep "P2P," not "press release" at the top of your mind.

There are lots of success stories and case studies documenting business success through Twitter. Here are a few of my favorite ways to leverage this platform for new business benefits.

1) Using Twitter search and other simple listening tools, monitor real time conversation about your brand that can assist your marketing and management teams in seeing what is really being about your company today. Modify your efforts based on the monitoring.

2) Perform real-time searches about your industry including competitor activity – you can see what is being said on Twitter about them. There are a variety of free and effective "listening" tools available to allow you to save searches such as Tweetdeck and HootSuite. One heating and air conditioning company had their best year ever simply by monitoring tweets about broken home systems and offering their prompt help.

In a legendary Twitter story, well-known blogger Heather Armstrong, who had just purchased a new washing machine to keep up with the diapers of her propitiously-pooping newborn, discovered that her $1,300 appliance didn't work. After several weeks of botched service calls, Heather vents on Twitter: "So that you may not have to suffer like we have: DO NOT EVER BUY A MAYTAG. I repeat: OUR MAYTAG EXPERIENCE HAS BEEN A NIGHTMARE."

After a few similarly-scalding messages, the magic began. She received messages from Maytag competitors offering help. Then she received a phone call from an executive at the Maytag corporate office who contacted an alternate repairs service, had the appropriate parts over-nighted, and had the machine repaired in less than a day. And competitor Bosch offered to give her a free washing machine, which she accepted and donated to a local shelter.

For many businesses, you MUST be listening on Twitter!

- It's where your customers are (and that includes B2B)
- It's where your customers speak to you (and the rest of the world too)
- If you don't listen and respond, your competitors will!

3) Offer helpful links and headlines that can drive traffic to your website, blog, landing pages, YouTube channels. Facebook, etc. Despite the social media hype, your website is usually the place where you ask for money... or registrations, downloads, or whatever you're after. Websites are still important in the social information eco-system.

4) Improve customer service by picking up conversations about your company that you might not be aware of and respond quickly to shut down any impending service or potentially damaging PR disasters. A friend of mine in Canada actually specializes in this -- monitoring the social buzz for impending strikes or disturbed company employees.

5) Having a hard time making that business connection through cold calls and email? Try a tweet or direct message. You will not believe how well this works. They may not return your calls but they almost always return tweets! I don't know the psychology behind this. I only know it works!

6) Run special deals and promotions on Twitter that you can use to drive traffic or move slow-moving stock. If you've don e a good job surrounding yourself with targeted connections, they should be interested in your specials, right? A local bakery is using this idea to move their products quickly if they've baked too much of a certain item that day

"come by before 4 p.m. for 2 for-1 coffee cakes." Hey, coffee cakes would certainly be meaningful content in my estimation! Especially cinnamon.

7) Twitter is an exceptional way to build your personal brand beyond your normal business borders. Even if you hit the speaking tour for a few months, the potential for global reach through Twitter probably has more potential... with a lot less wear and tear. Through Twitter, I even have name recognition among marketing thought leaders in Estonia -- which is a very friendly country I hear! How else could I have achieved a broad global following for my brand in a matter of months?

8) We've already discussed how directories such as Twellow can be used to find targeted followers. And by followers, I also mean "sales leads." LinkedIn has an outstanding advanced search capability -- you can find people by company, title, location, and other fields. You can even find their (drum roll) Twitter handle! LinkedIn has extremely limited ways to engage with folks and they might not "friend" a stranger on Facebook, but most people will engage with you -- even if you're unknown -- on Twitter.

9) By following potential customers, you can learn a lot about them, which will help you "pre-populate" the business relationship should you meet the person. I once recognized a stranger at a meeting because they looked just like their Twitter picture. Although a complete stranger to me, when I introduced myself he greeted me like a long-lost brother. He felt he knew me through my Twitter posts. Now, how many cold calls would you have to make to get a reaction like that?

10) Did you know Twitter can help your visibility on search

engines such as Google? Well you do now! Just a few years ago, search results would only turn up websites. Now you're just as likely to get LinkedIn profiles, video and yes, Twitter profiles.

11) Use your tweets as promotional testimonies. Tweets are published and permanent so feel free to use them as marketing tools. An example: One college featured real tweets about their school on an electronic highway billboard (not real-time of course!). A coffee shop featured happy customer tweets on a flat-screen display in their shop.

12) As people send nice tweets about you, save them in your "favorite" Twitter function. When you need to pull out customer testimonies, simply direct them to your Twitter page. This is public information for all to see.

13) The PR opportunities are significant. Journalists are extremely active on Twitter, seeking information on leads and sources. You might get some unexpected PR placements if you establish yourself as a voice of authority on Twitter.

14) I love the way businesses are using Tweet-ups -- networking meetings of Twitter enthusiasts -- to effectively promote their organizations. Twitter loyalists love to get together to meet in real life -- especially if there is free food involved. If you have an appropriate meeting space or venue, why not sponsor a Tweet-up to introduce folks to your facility while giving them a friendly place to meet? I think this would be effective for restaurants and clubs, banks, non-profits, schools, health clubs, real estate offices -- almost any place with a large meeting space that serves local clients.

15) I've touched on the personal opportunities to use Twitter as an educational device, but what if you turned this into

a competitive weapon for your entire organization? What would be the implications if your employees had access to real-time news and market information that your competitors don't have? I think it would be a good idea for you to buy copies of this book for every employee in your company. Heck, why not buy two!

16) Customer service is a popular use of Twitter by companies and other organizations but are topics too involved to get into in a meaningful way within the scope of this book. There are many well-documented best practices you can find by doing an Internet search on the topic.

Every day I'm learning about more and more creative uses for Twitter but these are a few of my favorites. I think these examples illustrate the potential and the diverse uses of Twitter as a legitimate business networking tool.

I know you're probably so excited to try some of these new ideas out that you can hardly wait to finish the book!

But wait a minute... what's that loud vacuuming sound I hear? Why it's Twitter sucking all your time away! This is a reality you're going to face all-too-soon. Twitter can take a ton of time, and it can also be fun and addictive. So let's tackle the issue head-on by providing a few actionable ideas to keep this thing under control.

Twitter Time-Savers

"How much time should I spend on Twitter?" is a question I get asked repeatedly.

There's no absolute answer to that question, just like there is no good answer to how much money a company should spend on advertising or how many resources should be devoted to research. It is completely dependent on the competitive structure of your field.

The time needed to do social media marketing right is a significant obstacle for many organizations. Part of the reason for this is that the duties are frequently piled on top of already-full plates at work. That's not fair, it's not smart, and it's not going to work as a long-term strategy.

Instead I'd like to have you re-think your entire approach to marketing and how new channels like Twitter fit in. Your customers are probably spending more time on social networking sites and less time on email, trade shows, and journals. Maybe it's time to re-think how you split your entire budget.

Like most people it took time and a few successes before I realized that Twitter should be considered a legitimate business tool. I get out of it more than I put into so the equation works for me. What will work for you? Let me suggest a minimum of 20 minutes a day.

I've divided this section into two categories — how you should spend 20 minutes a day for beginners and then the same approach for more experienced Twitterati.

The 20-minute Regimen for Beginners

In a world focused on "engagement" and "conversation" I'm going to give some unconventional advice — Forget about it for a few weeks. If you're a beginner and can only spend 20 minutes a day on Twitter, concentrate on Tao Lesson Number One: Building a relevant tribe of followers for the reasons we've already covered.

So in the first two months, tweet at least once a day so people see that you're active, but spend most of your time finding and following interesting people. Don't worry if they follow back or not. That will come in time. Building a targeted tribe is the prerequisite to any future success.

Now for the other half of your time, spend it reading, and occasionally responding to, tweets from your new friends. This will give you the chance to see what kind of tweets you like, which is instructive when you start tweeting more heavily yourself.

The 20-minute Challenge for Pros

Let's face it, if you're really immersed in Twitter, the challenge is probably how to not spend ALL your time on this addictive little channel! Once you have surrounded yourself with an interesting tribe, it's easy to "go down the rabbit hole" and follow link after interesting link.

Now that you have built up a critical mass of followers, it's time to take advantage of this amazing resource and engage and build meaningful connections, the second lesson of Tao. Here are a few time-saving corner-cutters:

- Get in the habit of sharing on Twitter every time you're reading on the Internet.
- If you're only spending 20 minutes a day on Twitter, do it at different times of the day so you have the chance to interact with a broader range of people.
- By now you're using some kind of an organizing tool like TweetDeck or HootSuite, right? It's an excellent way to improve your efficiency by helping you focus on those who are actively connecting with you.
- One of the most time-efficient Twitter strategies is to look for opportunities to re-tweet posts. This covers two bases at one time -- you're providing interesting and meaningful content and connecting with a follower too.
- Use a utility like ping.fm to post information on Twitter, Facebook, LinkedIn and other platforms simultaneously.
- Another great time-saver is using a Twitter application for a smart phone. Use those idle minutes waiting to pick up the kids at school!

Can you keep up with everything going on in your Twitter stream? No way. Not even if you spent 10 hours a day! Being effective in 20 minutes a day means knowing how to use these time-saving tips and then having the discipline to prioritize.

Secrets of Influence on Twitter

The notion of "influence" is among the most-debated and emotional topics you can bring up among the Twitter crowd. Even trying to DEFINE influence will invite an argument! At the end of the day, as long as <u>you</u> are satisfied with the business benefits you're receiving from Twitter, what anybody else thinks is irrelevant.

Still, whether you're a business professional or simply an enthusiastic participant on the social web, we should all be aware of this increasingly important trend of automated social influence scoring and consider how it might impact our opportunities.

While you may abhor the idea of somebody judging or grading you on a daily basis, it's already happening so we shouldn't just ignore this trend.

Dozens of "social influence" scoring themes have emerged and they are already being used by major corporations to identify thought leaders and create new marketing initiatives.

All of these scoring systems keep their computations closely held -- that's their secret sauce -- so you will never read a definitive theory on how to improve your scores across the board. The factors are too different and ever-changing. One executive insider told me his company tweaks his formula every single day.

Like most approaches to the dizzying world of social media, the strategy for improving social influence is to focus on the basics that are under your control. And that leads us back to the path described in this book, The Tao of Twitter. Let's look at how your focus on connections, content and helpfulness will improve your chances for a more effective "social imprint" on any grading system.

Targeted Connections and Social Influence

Every scoring system has some accounting for the number of followers, the "quality" of your followers, or both. The fundamental follower strategies defined in this book should support these factors of influence. Using some of the techniques I've discussed, spend time building a targeted, relevant audience. While some pundits will tell you numbers don't matter, I've already shown you that they do. More connections = more opportunities for business benefits.

Remember to cull your followers by blocking obvious spammers. Why is this so important to influence scoring?

Let's say I have 250 Twitter followers in my targeted and relevant audience. These people are more likely to engage with you through tweets, re-tweets, and recommendations to others than spammers only interested in building lists or broadcasting get-rich-quick schemes.

For example, if I send out a tweet and it's re-tweeted or commented on by 15 people, that's an engagement ratio of 6 percent.

Now let's say Mr. Bigshot Twitter King has 1,000 followers but only half of them are even real people. He never bothered to look at who is following him and is more interested in the appearance of a large number of followers. If he sends out the same tweet as me, it may attract some form of engagement from 50 people. Wow, that seems like it generated a lot of influence compared to 15 in the first example!

But let's look a little closer. Considering his large number of followers, Mr. Bigshot Twitter King had an engagement ratio of only 5 percent. On a percentage basis, he had less influence on his audience because most of followers aren't even real. By most social influence systems, he would receive less credit over time for this level of influence!

Taking the time to nurture and curate a quality list of followers takes extra effort but in the long-run it will provide benefits in terms of social influence.

You need both quality engagement and quantity of followers to ultimately be successful.

Meaningful Content and Social Influence

The core measure of most scoring systems is an ability to show how many people react to your tweets and how often.

That means you better be tweeting out something special! That's why providing consistent and compelling content is important. Can you see how this goes hand-in hand with focusing on a targeted and relevant community? If you surround yourself with people likely to be interested in you, they're going to be more likely to engage with you and your content. The more they engage, the more you are demonstrating to these scoring systems that you are influential.

Remember our little friend bit.ly, the helpful tool to "snip" URLs? Here's a trick to also let it help you measure and increase the level of engagement you receive.

One of the advantages of bit.ly is that it saves all of your links and displays how many times those links were clicked (even by time of day). It's almost like observing your audience "voting" on your content.

By doing a few experiments with different types of content at different times of the day and different days of the week, you might see a pattern of content that is the most popular.

After you've been on Twitter for awhile, you will certainly get an intuition about what content generates engagement by the instantaneous feedback of replies and retweets.

Authentic Helpfulness and Social Influence

Another aspect of social influence is also WHO is engaging with you. If you are influencing the influencers, you're more influential. That sentence might make you a little dizzy but I think it makes sense, right?

This can be a tricky business. How do you get busy people -- maybe even with a bit of a celebrity ego -- to even follow you, let alone engage with you?

The answer comes through your conscientious efforts to be helpful. If you're helpful, kind, and useful, you'll be much more likely to appear on somebody's radar screen.

You might be wondering how you can even tell if somebody is

influential or not. More and more, standard Twitter applications like HootSuite (more on this later) display an influence score right in the user profile.

Here are a few tips to get noticed by influential connections:

- If you see an influencer online, say hello to them through a tweet or send them a compliment.

- Re-tweet their content, especially if it is something of vital interest to them like their business, their blog, or a favorite charity.

- If they have a blog, comment on it. Bloggers love comments in their community and will usually pay attention to anyone who takes the time to contribute. This will make them much more likely to recognize and respond to you in the Twitter stream.

- Pay attention to their tweets and show helpfulness. For example, if an important potential business contact or thought leader mentions they are going to be in Boston, and you know of a favorite restaurant in Boston, let them know. Now that's a tweet that will get their attention!

- Another technique is to find commonality. Look through their LinkedIn profile for a common hometown, friend, place of employment, or college. Then find a way to mention this coincidence in a tweet.

- Ask them a direct question. While people may be busy, in general the most influential people on Twitter got there by following The Tao of Twitter, too. They can't resist an opportunity to be authentically helpful. So if you ask a question or ask for help, you're more than likely to get a response unless it's a Hollywood type.

Finally I want to emphasize the AUTHENTIC part of Authentic Helpfulness. The social web tends to amplify personal characteristics. If you're just trying to use people to make a sale, it's going to come across and define your reputation and personal brand. If you're generous and gracious without expecting anything in return, people will go out of their way to look out for you.

Trust the Tao and be patient. It WILL happen.

Advanced Twitter Concepts

Believe it or not, your Twitter journey is just beginning. This section contains some advanced concepts to help you get even more benefits from the platform. It would be a good idea to take a month or even two to master the basic concepts of The Tao before jumping into these ideas. But if you have a handle on it, here are some new things to try out.

Audience Maintenance -- When your tribe grows beyond a few hundred people you will probably want to clean out some of the people who are not following you, or those who have become inactive. There are lots of free applications to do this but it's a rapidly-changing scene. My recommendation is to do a Google search or even a Twitter search for "Twitter maintenance applications" and find suggestions on the best available applications.

Custom Backgrounds -- As you explore Twitter you'll notice that many people have customized their Twitter home page to include interesting backgrounds and relevant business information.

These range from free pages to low-cost websites that allow you to customize your site. It's a good idea to provide business information this way by doing a Google search for "Twitter backgrounds" and finding a service that fits your need and budget. Keep these guidelines in mind:

- This will communicate about your brand so make sure it reflects well on your business
- Don't make it look too much like an advertisement
- Include other ways to connect with you such as LinkedIn and Facebook
- At this time, Twitter pages do not link to websites
- Consider having a local graphic designer do a custom page for you. Find some pages that you like as examples so they have something to go by. You can usually have a custom site done for you for under $200.

Geolocation or Geotagging -- The use of location data in Tweets to tell us where you are in real time. Is also called "Tweet With Your Location." This is an option in your settings and can be used by certain applications to identify Twitter followers near you. I personally think this crosses a line on privacy and don't recommend using this option.

Influence -- There are several fun applications that will allow you to "grade" your Twitter effectiveness and even compare it to others. Twitter Grader is a popular utility for this. Klout is a pioneer in the area of social influence scoring. Don't get too caught up in your score. Remember your business goals! Stick to the fundamentals of The Tao and you will be fine.

Legal Implications -- Publishing on Twitter creates a permanent and searchable record of your statements. While it's important to be real, it's also important to be careful. My favorite local pizza proprietor was sued for $2 million after posting an unflattering tweet about his advertising agency.

In a corporate environment, lawyers should be involved in determining the social media policy to account for laws and regulations specific to your industry.

I'm not suggesting that you become paranoid, but just be aware that you're always publishing.

Listening Platforms -- Once you get above about 300 followers, it becomes increasingly difficult to follow the conversations. You'll be facing a daily wall of noise. At this point you need to bring in help by downloading a free or low-cost "listening" platform to organize your conversations.

Some of the leading names in this space include Seesmic, Tweet-Deck, and HootSuite. I've already mentioned these tools as a way to schedule tweets, save searches, and cut corners on time.

But the primary advantage of these applications is that you can divide your followers into logical groups. For example, you might have one called "industry experts" and another called "local friends." That way you can isolate and segment the people you REALLY want to listen to and follow their conversations. These apps also have the ability to save searches so you can see a stream of targeted information of interest to you. There are also other little tricks built into these apps to make it much easier and fun to follow along on Twitter. All have versions for smartphones and the iPad.

Mobile -- All major smart phone platforms have free Twitter apps available. This way you can carry Twitter with you wherever you go... and you'll want to. They all provide the opportunity to snap a photo from your phone and attach it to a tweet. This can be a lot of fun to share with your friends! There are multiple platforms available in smartphone app stores or download a mobile version of your desktop listening platform.

Twitter Blog -- Twitter is constantly changing and improving. To keep up with the latest ideas, I recommend following the Official Twitter blog to stay current on best practices.

Twitter Chats -- There are regularly-scheduled chats on many industry topics usually identified by a hashtag designation. A list can be found here: http://bit.ly/9zAZrR. Chats on Twitter can be followed using an app like TwitterFall or Twit Chat. Even with these utilities, many people have a hard time following the rapid-fire chat style on Twitter. Still, this is a great way to interact with people and also find relevant, targeted people to follow.

Social Media Policies -- Earlier I suggested that companies can deploy the use of Twitter throughout an organization as a possible competitive advantage. But what constitutes abuse? How much time should employees spend on social media at work? What if employees access inappropriate sites?

All of these questions and much more should be addressed in a social media policy. Every company should have a policy -- even if employees can't access the social web via company computers, it's likely they are getting online through their smart phones. In one news story, a teacher was disciplined for a comment she made about a student on a site unrelated to the school. So to be fair to everybody, make sure employees know what's expected, and what's at risk.

Here's a website with hundreds of examples of organizational social media policies:

http://socialmediagovernance.com/policies.php

Spam -- By mid-2009 Twitter was becoming so overrun by hackers and spammers that the service was teetering on being unusable. The company has done a good job cleaning up its act but the spammers are always coming up with new tricks.

"Spamming" can describe a variety of different behaviors. Here are some common tactics that spam accounts often use:

- Posting harmful links (including links to phishing or malware sites)
- Abusing the @reply or @mention function to post unwanted messages to users
- Creating multiple accounts (either manually or using automated tools)
- Spamming trending topics to try to grab attention
- Repeatedly posting duplicate updates
- Posting links with unrelated tweets
- Aggressive following behavior (for instance, mass following and un-following in order to gain attention)

It would be difficult to provide complete guidelines because the tactics change so often. The problems are usually more in the category of annoying versus dangerous, but you should still actively report undesirable behavior for spam. This action doesn't immediately or definitely cause an account to be suspended, but it's an important tool Twitter uses to identify and investigate spam accounts.

Verified Accounts -- On certain accounts (especially celebrities) you'll see a little blue check mark next to the user name. This means that account is the real person. It's so easy to set up fake accounts that this has become necessary for some people who are in the public spotlight.

Is Twitter for Everybody?

This is the big question that eventually gets asked by every person and every company trying Twitter for the first time. In the height of your initial frustrations, you may be wondering ... is Twitter really for everybody?

Most consultants will tell you "yes." Indeed, there is probably some business use or benefit available for everyone and every organization.

But after working with hundred of business professionals across many diverse businesses, I've come to realize the answer is no -- it's not for everyone.

Here's an example. One of my customers is a brilliant management consultant. An engineer by training, he does not come by marketing instinct naturally and asked me to help.

This is a customer who would be <u>perfect</u> for Twitter:

- Small business-owner
- Enormous, global market potential (needs a lot of awareness)
- Small marketing budget
- Selling differentiated personal services
- No time to blog, develop extensive content, etc.
- Tech-savvy
- Is a charming, bright person with engaging personality.

And yet he WILL NOT TWEET. I coaxed, cajoled, and threatened him. I've trained him patiently and even prescribed a daily Twitter regimen. I demonstrated the power of the platform when I found him a potential new business contact on the very first day of our operation. He didn't follow-up and seems content with his tweet-free existence.

This may seem strange, but it isn't uncommon. I've found similar resistance from many people who can obviously benefit from this business tool. I asked my client "why" and here is his answer:

"I'm not sure why really. I guess the idle chatter (which is mostly what I seem to see when I log on) just doesn't make any sense to me. There's obviously some self-imposed barrier that I can't or just don't want to cross. You were kind enough to introduce me to Twitter, and I appreciated that. There's the old expression about leading a horse to water. Guess I'm just not that thirsty for Twitter water... at least yet."

This type of reaction is not unusual. In fact I was a Twitter Quitter myself and had to really push through a few weeks of this non-intuitive communication platform before I started to understand it.

What is the difference between a Twitter-lover and hater? Does success on Twitter lend itself to a certain personality type? Some say it favors out-going people, yet introverts are quick to say that they love the platform as way to connect on their own terms and build quality relationships their own way. Maybe it has something to do with patience. Perhaps it is being creeped out by the crowds or by having strangers "follow you."

Honestly, I haven't figured it out, but I do acknowledge the fact that some very intelligent and wonderful people just don't like Twitter even when they can see the benefits. So be it.

What About Organizations?

Is there a business case for Twitter for every organization and company? Like nearly every business question, the answer is, "It depends!"

Medical professionals, lawyers, financial managers, and defense contractors may have severe regulatory limitations on the information they can discuss in public. Remember, Twitter is a form of publishing.

When it comes to business communications strategy, it really gets down to this: What are your business objectives? What do you need to say? Where do your customers get their information?

If your customers are not engaging in this platform you're going to waste a big wad of time on Twitter and get frustrated.

But I want to suggest two big HOWEVERs before you decide your business is not cut out for Twitter.

HOWEVER, you may not really know where your customers are getting their information, even if you <u>think</u> you do! People are piling on to the social web in record numbers and are also spending an enormous amount of time there. In an always-connected world, the role of social media in the business and personal world is blurring.

I had a client who resisted Twitter because she insisted that her customers had no interest in it. I conducted some customer research for her -- completely unrelated to Twitter -- and discovered that "social media" was the number one marketing and business issue for the majority of her customers! By getting in front of the curve and mastering Twitter before her customers were immersed in it, she was able to guide them, position herself as a subject matter expert, and even create some new business opportunities for her company.

Now for HOWEVER number two -- However, there are MANY other business benefits to Twitter beyond simply getting sales leads. Even if your customers aren't there in force, it is still an incredibly powerful way to learn, connect with thought leaders, and identify new business opportunities.

I have seen an array of diverse organizations thrive on Twitter, from pizza joints to florists, from mega-brands to my handyman (who I found on Twitter). Colleges, hospitals, non-profits, realtors, health professionals, shipping companies, government agencies, and utilities have all realized business gains from a Twitter presence.

There's a reason I placed this chapter near the end of the book. By now you have learned about the transformational power of this platform and have read some inspiring success stories. It's not so hard to quit now is it? There are just so many way to define success, create wealth, discover benefits, and even have fun with Twitter.

OK, let's put it all together.

Putting It All Together

One night I was observing a Twitter conversation going back and forth between a woman named Amy Howell (@howellmarketing) and several marketing professionals in my tribe.

Amy seemed enthusiastic (uses lots of !!!), supportive, intelligent and fun. From her professional and complete Twitter profile, I could tell she runs a public relations and marketing firm in my home state of Tennessee. The link to her website also showed me that we share many interests and she is a fellow blogger. Perhaps there were opportunities for synergy?

Amy and I had connected -- we were following each other on Twitter -- but we had not really CONNECTED. She seemed like a person I would like to get to know and possibly even do business with so I made a conscious decision to get to know her. Over the next few weeks I...

- Looked for opportunities just to say hello and compliment her when I saw her online.

- Read her tweets and, when I saw interesting content, re-tweet it to my followers.

- Started reading her blog, commented on it, and in an act of authentic helpfulness, tweeted a link to her blog to the people who follow me. This helped promote her efforts.

Soon, Amy and I were having regular conversations over Twitter. We grew to like each other and she appreciated the support I gave her by tweeting her links and blog posts. She started to return the favor and quickly became an online friend and loyal reader of my blog.

As I often do, I invited my new Twitter friend to talk on the phone. In this age of conversation-avoidance, a phone call seems like a luxury but I think it is an essential part of building strong new business relationships, especially if a live meeting is improbable.

In our call Amy mentioned that she had an upcoming meeting in Knoxville and that she wanted to stay overnight to have dinner with me and my wife. I couldn't have been more pleased and excited to finally meet my new friend.

But a conflict arose. I had committed to a speaking engagement at a regional marketing meeting and the time of the event was moved to the exact day Amy was to be in town. I had an idea -- wouldn't Amy make a great addition to the panel discussion? Everyone agreed and Amy became an important part of the program, giving her the chance to network with a host of new relevant business professionals.

After the event, we had dinner and Amy mentioned she was part of a group of fellow marketers and bloggers called the Social

CMO. The group was going to attend a conference she was planning in Memphis and meet to discuss ways to work together. I was very interested and shortly, through Amy's recommendation, I became part of the group.

On my way to the Memphis meeting, I had to drive through Nashville during the traditional lunch hour in the U.S. I had started to connect on Twitter with a young woman named Laura Click (@lauraclick) who lived in that city and, although I did not know her very well, invited her to meet for lunch. Laura and I hit it off and the meeting started an important business relationship for me -- Laura has since helped me with client writing assignments, contributed a guest blog post, helped me write a chapter for a book and collaborated on a charity effort. I also helped her become a member of The Social CMO.

When I arrived in Memphis I was fortunate to meet many Twitter friends for the first time. One of them was Glen Gilmore (@glengilmore), a well-known New Jersey attorney and one of Amy's strategic partners. Months later I was in a position to recommend my new friend Glen for a teaching position at his alma mater, Rutgers University -- a thrill for both of us.

I also got to meet dozens of other thought leaders like Jeremy Victor (@jeremyvictor), Billy Mitchell (@billymitchell1) and Ryan Sauers (@ryansauers) who have become close friends and collaborators.

Amy and I continue to find business opportunities for each other and partner in many ways... and we always will.

By now, I hope you can see this important pattern of connections, content and authentic helpfulness running through all of these success stories. And as you continue to learn I'm sure you will see this theme everywhere on the social web.

And while it has created surprising and amazing benefits, in the long term the most important pay-off will be the relationships I've formed with Michelle, Trey, Nathan, Aaron, Amy, Laura, Glen and hundreds of other folks who follow The Tao of Twitter.

I want to end this book the same way I end all of my social media marketing classes -- with a quote from an unknown university student who left this comment on my blog:

"Social media marketing is not something that can be taught -- it has to be experienced and this is why schools have a hard time teaching classes about it. Students who take advantage of social media will have a leg up on those who do not. Formal education and books can show you the tools... but it is up to you to learn how to apply them for you and your business."

I'm so grateful that you've read my book. But no matter how many times you return to it, you can't master The Tao of Twitter until you immerse yourself in it and learn by doing. So I want to encourage you to be persistent, patient and present.

Best of luck as you find your own path, your own Tao, on your lifetime Twitter adventure.

Acknowledgements

The story of any Twitter journey is one of friendships. I have dozens of wonderful tales about hundreds of people I could have included in this book. My love and deepest respect goes out to my Twitter Tribe, students, and customers. You have changed my life in amazing ways.

Nancy Guertin designed the beautiful interior elements of this book. I met her through a Twitter connection.

Carrie J. Bond has been such a support in many ways as I wrote this book, including proof-reading. She was my best friend in kindergarten ... and re-connected with me through Twitter.

To my offline family, Ryan, Lauren, Avery, and Hannah. Thank you for your support and patience while I was buried in my laptop. Their role in my life had nothing to do with Twitter.

My dear love Rebecca, the queen of my life -- Thank you!

About the Author

Mark W. Schaefer's blog {grow} can be found at www.businessesGROW. com and is one of the best-loved business and marketing blogs in the world. His work has been featured in popular and academic journals across many disciplines.

Mark has nearly 30 years of experience in PR, sales and marketing with a variety of businesses from Fortune 100 companies to start-ups. He has seven international patents for his business innovations and advanced degrees in marketing and applied behavioral sciences.

Mark is currently executive director at his own marketing consulting company, Schaefer Marketing Solutions and teaches at several colleges and universities, including the graduate studies program at Rutgers University in the United States.

Follow Mark on the web:

Twitter   @markwschaefer
Facebook   http://on.fb.me/markwschaefer
LinkedIn   http://linkd.in/mwschaefer
YouTube   http://bit.ly/yt-schaefer

CPSIA information can be obtained at www.ICGtesting.com
Printed in the USA
LVOW110943180312

273583LV00001B/65/P